Learning
to

Learn

...A sure-fire way to improve your academic performance!

Claire Odogbo

Order this book online at www.trafford.com
or email orders@trafford.com

Most Trafford titles are also available at major online book retailers.

Printed in Victoria, BC, Canada.

ISBN: 978-1-4269-2897-0

Our mission is to efficiently provide the world's finest, most comprehensive book publishing service, enabling every author to experience success. To find out how to publish your book, your way, and have it available worldwide, visit us online at www.trafford.com

Trafford rev. 4/13/2010

 www.trafford.com

North America & international
toll-free: 1 888 232 4444 (USA & Canada)
phone: 250 383 6864 ♦ fax: 812 355 4082

This book is dedicated to all those who have a thirst for learning and a desire to learn more effectively.

Acknowledgements

To God, who is the true source of all inspiration for this book.

My husband Fidelis Odogbo, who gave me all the love and encouragement while he wondered what I was up to -writing and typing furiously,

My Sister, Sarah Uyovbukerhi, who edited this book,

Mina Ochoche, who ensured I had the time to complete this book by babysitting,

Alberta Stevens who encouraged me not to give up on this dream,

My baby Sophie, who made sure she slept so mummy can write-

Thank you all for your invaluable support.

You made this possible.

Table of Contents

Introduction

In the course of working with students across various disciplines, I have realized that many have problems with their studies because they have not understood the basic principles about learning.

Most teenagers and young adults in our schools and institutions of higher learning do not know how to learn. They are used to simply memorizing things without understanding them, and then providing the memorized information as their answers to relevant questions asked in tests and examinations.

Such a learning method creates a very weak foundation for true learning and development, as it does nothing to improve the learner.

This guide is an attempt to correct this problem and aid those who really wish to learn, along the path of true learning, to attain self-development and higher achievements in life.

How to use this manual

This manual is designed as a handbook for the person who wants to be a more effective learner.

Anyone who wishes to benefit from it must constantly refer to it in order to effectively implement the principles and ideas presented herein.

This work is designed for easy reading and comprehension by persons in the 7th grade and higher, hence the Author has refrained from delving too deep into the intricacies involved in learning. However, further research is encouraged by anyone who is interested in doing so.

All enquiries concerning the contents of this book should be addressed to the Author, via e-mail: elouyo@yahoo.com.

1

Your Unique Brain

The brain is the most unique, yet complex organ in the human body.

There is no computer that can function like the human brain. Indeed, all attempts to make such a computer has failed till date.

Five things your brain can do

- Store up 50 times more information than that contained in all the 9 million books of the library of congress in the United States of America.
- Can form up to 10^{800} of associations, that is, if written down in plain manuscript, over 10.5 Million Kilometres of associations or patterns.
- Can process thought faster than the speed of light.
- Can store and retrieve your experiences from childhood to maturity.
- Can understand, store and recognize patterns all at once (gestalt/grok)

The human brain is divided into two halves or sides, known as the left and right brains.

- The left side of the brain is responsible for our ability to learn, speak and understand language, and our aptitude for numbers, logic, sequence, attention to details, symbolic representations, and judgment.

- The right side of the brain is responsible for our ability to appreciate images, rhythm, music, imagination, colour, patterns, emotions and such like. It is that part of our brains that helps us see things as a whole, in a non-judgemental, unbiased way.

All the traits expressed through the left and right sides of the brain are critical to our thinking processes. It is the ability of both sides to constantly and successfully work together as one that brings about creativity in our thinking processes.

RIGHT SIDE
LEFT SIDE

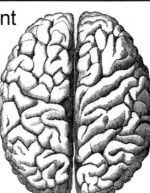

RIGHT SIDE
- Non Judgement
- rhythm
- music
- images
- imagination
- daydreaming
- colour
- dimension

LEFT SIDE
- Judgement
- language
- logic
- number
- sequence
- linearity

2

The Creative You

Every human being is born with a good measure of creative ability. Understanding yourself, your creative ability and how to use it correctly, is the secret of effective learning at any level of study.

Your talent may not be expressed in the things that people readily recognise as talent, but you do have it in you.

You must try to think deeply about yourself, the way your mind works, the way you act, react and generally do the things you do, in order to discover your area of special ability or talent, and how to develop it for use in every possible area of your life. This is creativity.

Creativity has been defined as, drawing new patterns from previously unassociated thought processes; and the generation of new ideas or concepts from previously existing ideas or concepts.

Thus the one who thinks of making shoes that can help people walk on water, for example, is exercising his mind creatively. Though he may get laughed at the moment he speaks of his ideas, he must not give up, for such unusual thinking is the road to extra-ordinary achievements.

For example, the Wright brothers who first thought of a machine to help people fly, were considered crazy and not worth any serious attention. But they kept on developing their ideas, and today their work has evolved into commercial and military aircrafts, spacecrafts, rockets and so on. What was once thought impossible is now achievable.

Having understood that we all have creative ability somewhere inside us, we must also understand that we are not all the same; therefore the way we express our creativity for others to see is different for each of us.

The reason for this difference lies in our personality, that quality in us that makes us do the things we do the way we do them.

Studies show that there are 16 personality types to which people may belong, ranging from the extreme introvert to the extreme extrovert.

These 16 personality types are a blend of two or more of the four major categories of personalities in existence today. These four are the Sensing Thinkers, Intuitive Thinkers, Sensing Feelers and Intuitive Feelers. As we examine these four types (adapted from http://www.thoughtfuled.com/assess_identify.php), examine yourself to discover the category to which you belong.

Once you understand your personality type, you will begin to feel more confident of yourself and your unique abilities without trying to be like anyone else.

The Sensing-Thinkers (ST) or Mastery Learners:

Sensing Thinkers are Realistic, practical, and matter-of-fact people. They are efficient and results-oriented, preferring action to words, and actual involvement to theory. They have a high energy level for doing things which are pragmatic, logical, and useful.

Approach to Learning:
Sensing-Thinkers like to complete their work in an organized and efficient manner. They tend to be neat, well-organized, and precise in their work. They have an appetite for work, need to be kept busy, and require immediate feedback.

They would rather do almost anything than remain in their seat listening to someone speak. They need to be actively doing something, need to see tangible results from their efforts, and need to be in control of their task.

Sensing-Thinkers prefer step-by-step directions when assigned a task, and become impatient if the instructions become long and involved. More than any other learner, they want to know exactly what is expected of them. They need to know what they have to do, how they are to do it, and when it is to be done. Sensing-Thinkers will often lose interest in an activity if it moves too slowly, or if they can see no practical use for it.

Sensing-Thinkers need clearly-structured environments focusing on factual mastery of skills and an opportunity to apply them to something practical or to demonstrate proficiency in the skill. They prefer assignments which have right or wrong responses rather than open-ended or interpretive ones. They are highly motivated by competition, learning games, grades, gold stars, and other rewards for a job well done.

2. The Intuitive-Thinker (NT) or Understanding Learner:

Intuitive Thinkers are theoretical, intellectual, and knowledge-oriented. They prefer to be challenged intellectually and to think things through for themselves. They are curious about ideas, have a tolerance for theory, a taste for complex problems, and a concern for long-range consequences.

Approach to Learning:
Intuitive Thinkers approach learning in a logical, organized, and systematic fashion, bringing organization and structure to people

and things. They take time to plan, organize ideas, and determine necessary resources before beginning work on an assignment.

Intuitive Thinkers prefer to work independently or with other thinking types and require little feedback until their work is completed. They do not like to be pressed for time. When working on something of interest, time is meaningless. They display a great deal of patience and persistence in completing difficult assignments if the assignment has captured their interest.

Intuitive Thinkers attack problems by breaking them down into their component parts. They like to reason things out and to look for logical relationships. Their thought processes follow a cause-and-effect line of reasoning. They are constantly asking, "Why"?; and their questions tend to be provocative. Their concern is for relevance and meaning.

Intuitive Thinkers are avid readers. Their learning is vivid, and therefore, abstract symbols, formulae, the written word, and technical illustrations are preferred sources for collecting data.

Intuitive Thinkers usually display an affinity for language and express their ideas in detail. Everything they touch turns into words, spoken or written. They enjoy arguing a point based on logical analysis. In discussion, they often play the role of "devil's advocate" (that is, to purposefully argue for an opposite point of view).

Intuitive Thinkers are also concerned about being correct. They strive towards perfection, are self-critical, and are upset by mistakes - whether their own or other people's.

3. The Intuitive-Feelers (NF) or Self-Expressive Learner:

Intuitive Feelers are curious, insightful, and imaginative. They are the ones who dare to dream, are committed to their values, are open to alternatives, and are constantly searching for new and unusual ways to express themselves.

Approach to Learning:

Intuitive-Feelers are eager to explore ideas, generate new solutions to problems, and discuss moral dilemmas. Their interests are varied and unpredictable, but they prefer activities which allow them to use their imaginations and do things in unique ways. They are turned off by routine or rote assignments and prefer questions which are open ended, such as "What would happen if...?"

Intuitive Feelers are highly motivated by their own interests. Things of interest will be done inventively well. Things which they do not like may be done poorly or forgotten altogether. When engaged in a project which intrigues them, time is meaningless.

Intuitive Feelers operate by an "internal clock", and therefore often feel constrained or frustrated by external rules or schedules.

Intuitive Feelers are independent and nonconformist. They do not fear being different and are usually aware of their own and others' impulses. They are open to the irrational and not confined by convention. They are sensitive to beauty and symmetry and will comment on the aesthetic characteristics of things.

Intuitive Feelers prefer not to follow step-by-step procedures but rather to move where their intuition takes them. They prefer to find their own solutions rather than being told what to do or how to do it. They are able to take intuitive leaps, and they trust their own insights.

Intuitive Feelers often take circuitous routes to solving problems and may not be able to explain how they arrived at the answer.

Intuitive Feelers are flexible in thought and action, and are thus highly adaptable to new solutions. They prefer dynamic environments with many resources and materials.

Intuitive Feelers, more than any other type, are less likely to be disturbed by changes in routine. They are comfortable working with a minimum of directions. Their work is sometimes scattered and may look chaotic to thinking types.

Intuitive-Feelers are often engaged in a number of activities at the same time and move from one to the other according to where their interests take them. Often, they start more projects than they can finish.

The Sensing-Feeler (SF) or Interpersonal Learner:

Sensing-Feelers are sociable, friendly, and people-oriented. They are sensitive to people's feelings—their own and others'. They prefer to learn about things that directly affect people's lives rather than impersonal facts or theories.

Approach to Learning:
Sensing Feelers take a personal approach to learning. They work best when emotionally involved in what they are being asked to learn.

Sensing-Feelers tend to be spontaneous and often act on impulse, (that is, they prefer to do things because it "feels right"). They are interested in people and like to listen to and talk about people and their feelings. They like to be helpful to others and want to be appreciated for their efforts.

Sensing-Feelers, more than any other type, enjoy personal attention. They need to feel relaxed, comfortable, and to enjoy themselves while they learn. They like to think out loud, to work with other students, to share their ideas, and to get the reactions of their friends. They greatly prefer co-operation to competition, and need assurance or praise when they are doing well. They are greatly influenced by the likes and dislikes of others. Many times, they may complete a task as a means of pleasing someone rather than because they are interested in the task itself.

Learning Styles

Apart from our personality types, we all have our preferences for learning, which may be very different from what is obtainable in any school curriculum or programme.

A person who will maximise their creative potential, especially in the academic setting, must discover his personal preferences and work these to his advantage.

Studies show that people typically learn in any of the following ways (partly sourced from www.medscape.com):

Table 1.

Learning Style	Characteristics	Suggested Learning Tips
Visual	Prefers written instructions rather than verbal instructions. Prefers to have written illustrations or photographs to view when receiving written or visual instructions. Prefers a timeline, calendar or some other similar diagram to illustrate the sequence of events. Observes all the physical elements in the learning environment. Remembers and understands through the use of diagrams, charts and maps. Studies materials by making notes and organizing them in outline form.	Make your notes into colorful outlines. Make use of colorful flash cards, to aid learning and recall. Use diagrams, charts and mind-maps when studying.

Learning Style	Characteristics	Suggested Learning Tips
Auditory	Remembers what they or others say quite well. Remembers best by verbal repetitions and saying things aloud. Prefers to discuss ideas that they do not immediately understand. Remembers verbal instructions well. Finds it difficult to work quietly for long periods of time. Easily distracted by noise, but also easily distracted by silence. Enjoys group discussions.	Listen to audio lectures. Read aloud. Join a study group. Read with light music (for example, classical music) as it helps stimulate creativity.

Learning Style	Characteristics	Suggested Learning Tips
Kinaesthetic	Remembers best through getting physically involved in what is being learned. Enjoys the opportunity to build/or physically handle the learning materials. Will take notes to keep busy but will not often use them. Finds it difficult to stay still or in one place for a long time. Enjoys hands-on activities. Enjoys using computers. Tends to want to fiddle with small objects when working or listening. Remembers what they do, what they experience with their hands or bodies.	Ensure you get involved in the learning material by working through the examples and problems on your own. Work through your study material as much as possible. Include frequent breaks when you are studying. Make use of computers and other audio visual programs in your learning process.

Learning Style	Characteristics	Suggested Learning Tips
Kinaesthetic	Enjoys using tools or lessons which require active participation. Can remember how to do things after doing it only once.	

A close examination of the learning styles and thorough comparison with your own traits or behavioural patterns while learning may reveal that you either have one learning type, or a combination of two or more in varying proportions.

Are you wondering why that colleague or school mate of yours who does a lot of partying, only attends classes, takes notes, and does not spend a lot of hours studying; still manages to top the class effortlessly? That person is probably an auditory learner.

Do you wonder why you never seem to catch everything during a class or seminar, except you are given the opportunity to work on it yourself or probably work through exercises at home? You are probably kinaesthetic.

If you are never able to get anything out of a class unless there are pictures, diagrams, illustrations, and other visual aids, you are probably a visual learner.

Identifying, understanding and working with your learning style will unlock your academic potentials and help you achieve what you never believed you could.

Combining Learning Style Preferences with Personality Types.

Having known your predominant learning style, you must understand how to make it work with your unique personality.

For example, knowing that you are a 'Sensing thinking', or mastery learner and you are also kinaesthetic means you would most likely appreciate learning key points, and solving problems, in order to be your best in your academics.

On the other hand, a 'sensing feeler' or an interpersonal learner who also happens to be auditory would appreciate group discussions and thrive academically when they discuss before exams.

Understanding Your Creativity: Your Timing Preferences

The biological clock in human beings and animals has never ceased to amaze scientists the world over, as it subconsciously regulates our sleep patterns and our energy patterns, such as when we are highly energetic and otherwise.

For many individuals, this means that they can function maximally at certain times of the day, while they just push themselves to get through at other times.

Morningness and eveningness

Where do you fit in?

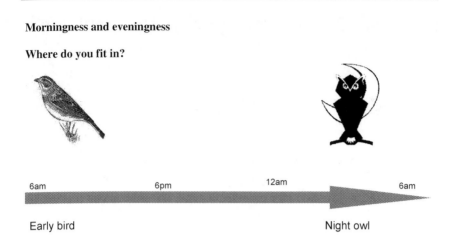

| 6am | 6pm | 12am | 6am |

Early bird   Night owl

Studies classify people according to two categories: Night owls (or Eveningness) and Early birds (Larks or Morningness).

They found out that for these two extremes, sleeping 2 hours later than usual can make a huge difference in their performance.

In America, studies have linked insufficient sleep to poor academic performance in high school children. Another study has linked sleep deprivation with a reduction in creative output.

Therefore, understanding your biological clock and arranging your schedule around it (in terms of your timing preferences) will put you ahead when preparing for a major event such as an exam, presentation or seminar.

Putting this to work: Timing Preferences

As a student, it is common practise to find people adopting a common timing preference for study, depending on your environment and your commitments. However, this does not necessarily work well for everyone.

According to one such student, in her first year in the university, all her colleagues studied primarily at night, so she joined in happily, not knowing that she was basically a day person. That year her grades were low, in spite of her efforts.

The next year she adjusted her study time to the day hours so she could sleep at night. From then on, her grades began to improve.

Everyone has a period of peak performance, when all your faculties are alert and functioning best. This period may not be same for everyone. You must discover your own period of peak performance and plan your study time within that period, as this will make a great difference between how much you will understand <u>and</u> remember from your study, and how much you don't understand or remember.

Personal Exercise to Determine your Optimal Learning Profile

On a sheet of paper write down the answer to the following questions:

1. When are you most active, Night or Day?

2. How do you like to learn? On your own or with other people (discussion group)?

3. When you run into a difficult math problem, which of the following do you do?
   a. Discuss with a friend.
   b. Try to solve until you find the solution.
   c. Research about the problem with some textbooks.
   d. Look for an alternative way to solve the problem.

4. Do you enjoy learning when you are actively involved or you prefer to sit back and listen?

5. When are you most happy when you are learning? When you see images and other illustrations or when you are listening?

6.You remember best a class that you:
 a. Listened to.
 b. Participated in.
 c. Saw images and other visual illustrations.

Compare your answers with the information on previous pages. It should tell you something about your timing preferences, learning style and personality. If unsure, contact the author.

3

Effective Learning

Learning, just like any other worthy endeavour, has a set of principles guiding its working. Many of us have got our fingers burned in this area simply because we have failed to understand the principles of learning and apply them successfully.

For example, in order to pass an exam, you have to read the material, study it, interpret It correctly to yourself, and gain a better understanding of the subject matter treated in that material, which can be easily remembered and applied.

Studies show that with the right techniques, even a person previously thought to be dull academically, will perform far above expectation.

If your primary language is different from the language in which lectures and study materials are presented, your first task must be to master the language of study, otherwise you cannot achieve any meaningful progress in that area.

The basic principles for effective learning involves developing the right input skills, process skills and output skills.

Table 2:

Input skills	Process Skills	Output skills
Note taking	Time management	Test/exam taking
Reading	Learning and memory	
Research	Exam and test preparation	
Class participation		

Input Skills

Note taking
Reading
Research
Class participation

Note Taking

The first skill a person needs in order to have good notes is effective listening.

As simple as it sounds, most people do not have good listening skills because they are not used to listening in their normal, everyday daily lives.

Each one wants to make his or her point heard first, and mostly only listen casually until they get the chance to say what they what is on their minds.

While the other party is talking, they spend the time thinking of what they want to say, and totally miss the information that has been communicated.

The same thing happens during note-taking. Many students are unable to take good notes because they are usually distracted by their classmates, or by thoughts of other things they want to do after the class. This makes them fail to listen intently enough to grasp the information being communicated by the teacher.

Such students often find themselves scrambling for the notes of other classmates whom they see as more intelligent than themselves, at the end of the class. Truth is, the good note takers are not always more intelligent than the bad note takers; they are just more focused at listening and learning during classes than the bad note takers. And because good notes are the foundation of good grades, the good note takers often come up ahead of the class.

So if your notes are always scanty and of little help during study, do not lose hope. You can take better notes by learning good listening habits.

One secret that will help you listen better in class, is to read anything you can find that is relevant to the subject or topic that will be treated in class. Doing this will make you more interested in what the teacher has to say, and increase your level of participation in the class.

Also, as you listen to what the teacher is saying, try to relate what is being said to what you already know about the topic of discussion, and try and answer any questions that you had when you were reading about the topic before the class.

Try to sit as closely as possible to the teacher, so that you can closely observe his or her facial expression and ask any questions you may have. Endeavour to ask your questions before the teacher leaves the class, so that you can add the answers to your notes.

Effective note taking does not mean that you must capture every single word spoken, so do not expect to take down every word from a lecture. Instead, write down the most important points. You would easily identify these if you had prepared by reading about the topic before the class.

Try to leave wide margins in your notes while taking them down (so you can add more information later), or have a personal study notebook for each course.

While in class, take note of questions asked by the teacher, as these often form the basis for possible test or exam questions. Also take note of questions involving what, who, where, when, why, and how. It may help to answer such questions during your study time at home.

Keep your notes safe, as these would form the base for your studies throughout the session.

After class, try to summarise the entire class in 6 to 9 key sentences.

Confucius reportedly said that the faintest stroke of a pen is longer than the longest memory. Therefore, even after mastering effective listening, you may forget what you heard if you do not capture those thoughts on paper before you forget them altogether. It is said that it takes only fifteen minutes to forget what we hear.

Reading

As easy as it seems, reading can be difficult, especially when preparing for an exam or test.

We suddenly realise how ill prepared we are when we face the question papers, and realise that although we have studied, we can not recall everything we read, enough to score our desired grade.

Most of us attribute this to having a poor memory, but this is usually not the case.

The real problem is poor reading skills. Most people have not learned to distinguish content reading from superficial reading. Most times we get deceived into thinking that we must read the book from cover to cover in order to get the most out of our study.

Surprisingly, this is not true, as reading from cover to cover tends to slow down our reading. This makes us miss out on the key information we need, which is wrapped up in all the information given in the book.

Educationists have taught that effective content reading should comprise the following:

1. **Survey** the text by skimming over the text to get a general feel of the material being studied.

2. Develop a series of **questions** based on the material that you have already surveyed, as this encourages reading for purpose.

3. **Recite** the answers to the questions that have been formulated.

4. **Revise** the material to ensure that you get the complete picture.

Remember that the aim of reading is to fish out the key messages from the maze of information given.

Tony Buzan, the major developer of brain technologies, has also proposed his method for highly effective study. I refer to this method as the fill- in- the –gap reading style, as you will see.

According to him, to effectively study, you must prepare for it first by doing the following:

- Browse through the book or content which you are about to study.

- Decide on the best use of time, how many hours you want to spend, when you want to spend it, and the areas of the material you wish to cover during that time.

Gather all the information you have about the subject by quickly jotting down everything you know about the subject. This should be done within 2 minutes maximum. This helps keep your mind from wandering and helps you focus on what you are about.

1. **Overview** the material by skimming through, taking note of the headings, graphs, illustrations and questions at the end of each chapter. This will give you a good idea of the

graphic sections of the book, and is quite different from merely skimming through. Try to convert your overview into a *mind map* (we will look at this later).

2. **Preview.** This involves covering the aspects not covered in the overview, such as the paragraphs. Some other educationists suggest that, at this stage you use the ***first, first, last*** method. In other words, read the first paragraph of each page, and then the first sentence of each paragraph and finally read the last paragraph. This is because writers usually put the most important information in the first paragraph and repeat this point in the concluding paragraph. At the end of this stage, include in your mind map the new information you have gathered from this stage.

3. **In-View.** The essence of this stage is to fill in the gaps of information left out in the first two stages. At this stage, pay special attention to difficult areas which you may have skipped during the previous stages. As before, add any new information to your mind map.

4. **Review** the material to gather any information not already captured in the three previous stages, and revisit any key areas you have identified while studying. Now complete your mind map.

This approach has proven to be more effective and creative because it encourages *personal involvement* or interaction with the material.

Time management in reading.

Most students find themselves gauging their hard work by the number of hours spent studying. This is not the correct way to determine the quality of study done, as one can spend ten hours reading, but realise that the real progress was achieved in only one hour of that time. The rest was spent in a struggle with a number of distractions, both within and without.

Therefore, to get more out of your study hours, break it down into small chunks of time – say 30 minutes each, with short breaks in-between.

This is recommended because we generally have a short attention span, and after 30 minutes our attention usually starts to stray to other things. Thus, you will find that after 30-45 minutes, your mind begins to wander until you realise that you are just turning the pages without really assimilating anything.

However, if you took a five minute break and did something different, like browsed through the news papers or magazine or listened to some music, you will come back to your books with renewed interest.

Another thing that you may try is this: if you are bored with a particular subject, take a break and read another subject, then return. The first subject which seemed boring or difficult will seem more interesting and easier by the time you return to it.

Research

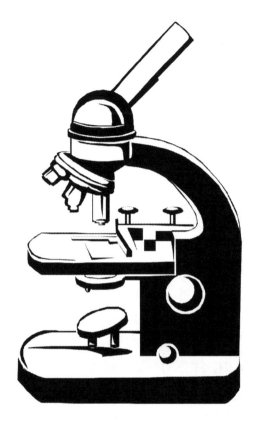

Research is an integral part of learning.

If you want to excel in your studies or at whatever you do, you should be able to approach whatever you are examining from different angles, as this helps give you a fresh perspective to your studies.

Research therefore becomes the spring board of new ideas and innovation.

The world wide web is a big source of information. With the internet within reach of almost everyone, we have more access to information and materials than at any other time in our history.

Sadly, only very few students know how to maximise the use of the internet to get the information they want.

Finding information on the internet is easy, with the use of special websites called search engines. Example of such search engines are www.google.com, www.msn.com, www.ask.com, and www.yahoo.com. There are hundreds more available, which cannot be listed here so the attention of the reader is not distracted.

Now to find information on the internet, open the search engine of your choice, and type in a keyword or phrase of the information you are looking for. Click go, or enter on your keyboard, and wait a few seconds. A list of options will appear. Click on each option to read its contents. If they include what you want, your search is complete. If they do not, go back and change the keyword or phrase and try again with the same or a different search engine. Repeating this will eventually bring up the information you want.

This process of getting information from the internet is known as 'surfing the web'.

It is extremely important to research class topics and information you are taught, as this will always put you ahead of your peers, and help you make intelligent contributions in class.

In addition, developing your skills in the area of research will improve the quality of assignments and term papers you submit in school, as it increases the clarity of your understanding and the ability to communicate that understanding effectively.

Class participation

This is perhaps one of the most over-looked but most important areas of study.

Many students avoid class participation due to the fear of rejection either from the teacher or from peers.

Students who have this fear must do everything they can to overcome it, because the extent of class participation will determine the level of excellence attained at the end of the term.

A careful observation will reveal that the students with the best grades are the ones who participate in class, as they use that opportunity to test their ideas and gain confidence in their reasoning and inferences.

If you are homeschooled or study via a distance learning program, all of this information may not completely apply to you, but you are strongly encouraged to adopt as much of it as will help you gain confidence in your own ideas and interpretations from your study material.

Process Skills

Time management
Learning and memory
Exam and test preparation

Time Management

Ever heard of the saying that "you can't eat your cake and have it"?

This sums up totally the principle of time management.

Many students underestimate the importance of how they spend their time until the exams are upon them, or the submission deadlines for assignments and projects have come. At this point they become stressed up and frantic, desperately trying to put something together to tide them over to the next level.

Thus you find otherwise brilliant students earning poor grades because they didn't take the time to do a good job while they had the chance.

If you are always behind schedule and never seem to have enough time in which to get all your work done, you need to take deliberate steps to manage your time.
There are many resources on time management, but the major guides will always stress on the need to prioritize your time.

There is a principle called the 80- 20 principle or Pareto's principle. It says that for many events, roughly 80% of the effects come from 20% of the causes.

When applied to time management, it means that in your day, only 20% of the things you want to do are a **must**. Identify these and handle them first. Every other thing falls into the secondary category of 80%, and must be treated only after the important 20% has been finished with. Doing things this way will help you achieve 80% effectiveness from attending to only the top 20% priorities in your day.

Other important tips are as follows:

No day in your life should be without its purpose. Assign each day several tasks and prioritize them.

Do not shy away from the most difficult tasks, do them while your energy is high, and tackle the easier ones later.

Develop a study timetable. This will ensure that you study every day. Break up your assignment or project into parts and assign a portion of it to yourself everyday, over a few days or weeks until it is complete. At the end, you would have achieved your aim. This is much better than trying to finish everything in one day, as this will only serve to discourage you from starting at all. As they say, the best way to eat an Elephant is to eat it a little at a time.

Minimise extra-curricula activities, and limit them to only those that you really must do, but remember to reserve some entertainment time for yourself, for "all work and no play makes Jack a dull boy".

Learn to say "no". This seems to be extremely difficult for many people, but it is one thing that saves people from many unpleasant things if they would dare to say it. Say "no" to anything that would take you off the course you have planned for your day, except it is very important.

Always carry a book or course material to read whenever you have a break, such as waiting for an appointment, a long bus or train ride, or waiting for lunch to be served.

Read something about time management monthly, as it keeps you aware of the need to manage your time effectively.

Finally and most importantly, kill procrastination, for it is the thief of time and killer of all good intentions.

Learning and Memory:

In discussing learning and memory, we shall revisit the human brain.

Here are some facts about your brain which are important for learning and memory:

The left Brain.
- Controls the right hand.
- Responsible for analysis, sequence, numbers, symbols, words, details and judgment.
- The majority are well schooled in the use of this as a result of the educational system.

Right Brain
- Responsible for Imagination, colors, rhythm, music, images, Looks at the whole, recognizes patterns, enhances non-judgment, and so on.
- Power house of creativity.
- Often stifled by our educational system, and thus used only by the minority.

The notes of some of the greatest geniuses that ever lived, such as Leonardo De Vinci show the active use of both sides of the brain.

This was the reason for their mental feats. Thus creativity is heightened when elements of both sides of the brain are allowed free expression.

Memory

The brain has capacity for acute memory and detailed recall.

- Ancient Greeks were renowned for their memory games and feats.
- Principles applied by these Greeks have been scientifically proven to be the key to a better memory.
- In order to tap into your potential for unlimited memory, the following principles must be observed:

a. Visualization: Anything the mind sees, it can remember. One picture is better than a thousand words. Picture anything you really want to remember.

b. Repetition: It is said that repetition is the law of lasting memory. To achieve this, repeat what you wish to remember again and again.

c. Reading out loud: This stimulates the brain via the ears to make connection with the subject you are trying to remember.

d.Association: This art is almost as old as man. The ancients learnt to remember facts by linking whatever needed to be remembered with a picture.

An ancient King, utilizing this technique was able to remember the names of his 300,000 strong army.

This technique has been used in our day and still produces the same results.

One of the best forms of associations is the picture-rhyme association.

This has led to the development of what is called the memory 'pegs' or 'hooks'.

The pegs or hooks don't change, but you can 'hang' just about anything on these hooks.

Several standard memory *hooks* exist. ***Their success lies in the fact that they rhyme with the numbers, for example tree and three, nine and dine.***

These hooks from numbers one to ten are as follows:

1. Bun	6. Sticks
2. Shoe	7. Heaven
3. Tree	8. Skate
4. Door	9. Dine
5. Drive	10. Pen

Bun

Shoe

Tree

Door

Drive

Sticks

Heaven

Skate

Dine

Pen

Application of Memory Hooks:

The idea behind the memory hooks is that they are supposed to be like hooks with which you hang up coats (or information) in your memory. You should learn them until you remember what these hooks represent for each number.

When you want to remember anything, create a mental picture associating the hooks to what ever you want to remember.

For example you wish to remember the following shopping list:

1. Butter
2. Cereal
3. Rice
4. Book
5. Dining set
6. Vegetables
7. Flowers

Now, using your memory hooks,
1. Imagine a picture of your bun sliced into two with your butter melted in between. Smell the melted butter in the hot bun.

2. Imagine drinking your cereal from a shoe-shaped ceramic dish. Imagine yourself struggling to get the last bit of cereal from the tip of your shoe dish.
3. Imagine a bag of rice, tied to a string hanging off your tree.
4. Imagine the book you want to buy at the foot of a door, or hanging off the door knob.
5. Imagine yourself driving a car with your dining set in the back seat.
6. Imagine the vegetables you want to buy growing off the tree sticks.
7. Picture your self in heaven with flowers all around.

If your imagination of these things are strong enough you will remember your shopping list easily enough. To achieve this clarity, it is advisable to close your eyes and see this image as clearly as possible.

You can also apply this number- rhyme principle to lists, when studying. Just associate as much information as possible with your hooks, and you will remember.

Remember, the more of your senses you involve in memorising anything, the better your recall.

According to Tony Buzan, the more of the following you incorporate in your picture, the more you will remember:

1. Exaggeration: The more exaggerated the image, the more you will remember.
2. Moving: As much as possible, make the image something that moves, preferably 3- dimensional.
3. Coloured: It should be brightly-coloured and vivid.
4. Imaginative: Use your imagination and make it as creative and individualistic as possible.
5. Pure: Link only one item to the hook as much as possible.

Where creativity is concerned there is no 'right answer'. Suspend judgment as much as possible, or these principles of memory will not work.

Personal Memory Exercise

Associate this shopping list with the number hooks.

1. Milk
2. Soap
3. Note book
4. Pen
5. Pencil
6. Sugar
7. Salt
8. Shirt
9. Plate
10. Chicken

Test your recall 3 hours later.

Radiant Thinking

Most people believe that the brain functions in the same way that we write, i.e in a linear fashion. But scientific evidence has shown that the brain works in a way known as radiant thinking, much like the ripples made in water when a pebble is thrown in, or like the ever widening circumference of a spider's web. Packets upon packets of information are sent from our brains in this way.

When we order our information in any other way, we naturally work against the memory recall process of our minds. For example, in writing linearly, words that are relevant for recall (keywords) are dispersed about by irrelevant words. Thus the relationship between

the concepts is not plainly observed.

Keywords

It was discovered that the brain stores information in this radiant way by forming links with keywords.

Keywords are words which funnel out of themselves, the same information funneled into it. It possesses "hooks" which in turn hook on to other words and so forms an endless chain of linkages.

These key words are usually strong Nouns or Verbs, surrounded by adverbs or adjectives. Thus the mention of a keyword will initiate the recall of other words, and pictures linked to that keyword.

Exercise

The Key word bursts (Mind bursts).
The idea behind this exercise is to see how the brain forms links with concepts and ideas. In no more than one minute, list as quickly as possible 10 words which can be associated with the following concepts:

Love
Corruption
Family
Success
Health
Riches

Be sure to exercise with other keywords that come to mind as you go along.

The key word exercise will help you navigate through the maze of information stored in your brain. With constant use, you will find that you are able to form easier associations and come up with concepts and Ideas more easily. In other words, you will find it easier to 'think on your feet'.

Using the Whole Brain

Previous sections have talked about the human brain having two hemispheres and the specialties of each hemisphere.

We have discussed the laws governing exceptional memory, and the keyword concept.

We know that being a genius is all about integrating all these in your everyday activities.

A tool called mind mapping was developed to help achieve this integration.

Exercise

Write a 30 minute presentation on wealth creation.
Time allowed: 5 minutes.

Mind Mapping:

This is a graphic method that helps one connect thoughts and ideas by associating things to them.

It helps the individual to better organize their thoughts and 'see' their mind more clearly.

It applies the keyword concept by forming associations with key words, which in turn connect to other keywords, forming a kind of map, hence the name (mapping).

It also integrates the rules governing long lasting memory by incorporating the principles previously discussed (exaggeration, color, imagination, movement).

It aims to incorporate all the elements of the left and right brain as much as possible, to achieve a heightened sense of creativity and ability.

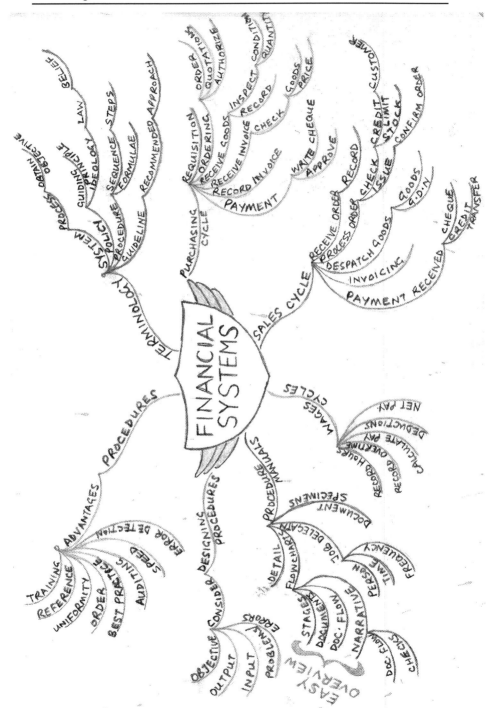

Mindmap of financial systems.

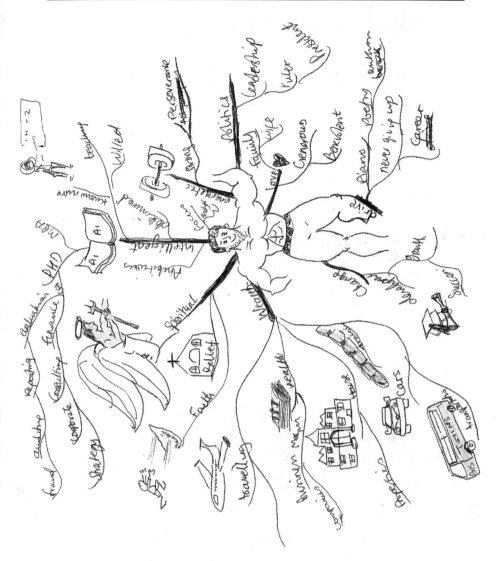

Mindmap on the life of a young man.

Applications of the Mind Map:

- Study
- Recall
- Presentation
- Planning
- Goal setting
- Project management
- Meetings
- Writing
- Brainstorming.

To create your own Mind Map:

- Place the key word you wish to map at the center. Highlight it so it catches the eye immediately.
- You may choose to place a circle or square around this key word.
- Let your basic ideas of this key word radiate from the center on thick branches.
- Let 'childlike' branches radiate from these other ideas till you have what seems like a web or tree.
- Use color throughout your mind map, for color stimulates memory.

- Place a plain sheet of paper in landscape orientation.
- Use single words as much as possible, and not phrases.
- Use images throughout your mind map.
- The more imagery and color your mind map has, the more 'magnetic' it is to memory.
- Eliminate judgment and leave your mind as 'free' as possible.

Exercises

Make a Mind Map around the following themes:

1. My self.
2. The Environment.

Applications of Mind Mapping

1. Recall

- Recall is easier with a mind map because you can 'see' the information in your mind's eye.
- Recall is also easier because you can easily highlight key words and establish patterns and relationships while using

a mind map, than any other learning method.

- Mind maps help summarize vast quantities of information in little time.
- A mind map helps you obey all the relevant laws governing memory, thus making the recall process easier and more fun.

2. Study

- Mind maps help reduce the pile of work to study.
- It makes study more fun, and helps you get more out of your study time.
- It helps to summarize tons of information (such as a lecture or manual) into more manageable units.
- It helps improve understanding.
- It improves confidence in your learning abilities as a result of better recall.

3. Writing and Communication

- Mind maps have proven to be a very useful tool in business and creative writing.

- Mind maps work well with the brainstorming principles.

- Placing whatever you want to write about as the subject of your mind map, helps you to quickly get the entire writing into perspective.

- Mind maps enable your mind to flow quickly on paper.

- Writing about a subject which you have first mind-mapped makes writing much easier, reducing the completion time by more than 60%.

- Writing from mind maps makes your writing richer and much more expressive.

4. Personal Development

- The brain is like a maze of information. Mind maps help to organize this maze into a useful resource.

- Using mind maps regularly will help you navigate through your mind to find answers much more quickly than before.

- Consequently, using mind maps frequently will cause an increase in productivity in every aspect of your person; and enable you to tackle projects, assignments and deadlines much more efficiently.

Applications of Mind Mapping: Using Mind Maps for Study and Recall.

The Learning Continuum.
Studies show that if unaided by repetitive study, the learning curve goes downward with the passage of time as shown in the diagram below:

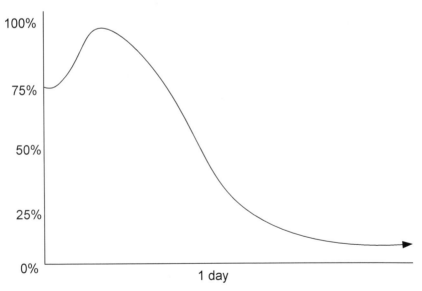

100%

75%

50%

25%

0%

1 day

Graph of amount of information recalled versus time lapse. Information recalled diminishes greatly with increase in time lapse.

Thus, lack of repetitive study, and not poor memory, is the main reason why most of us do not recall what we study.

However, through the use of mind maps, you can improve your recall during study sessions by reviewing your mind maps in the following order:

- After the first few minutes,
- After 24 hours,
- After 1 week,
- After 1 month,
- After 6 months, and
- After one year.

The effect of following this procedure is that you remember everything you have studied, as shown in the diagram below:

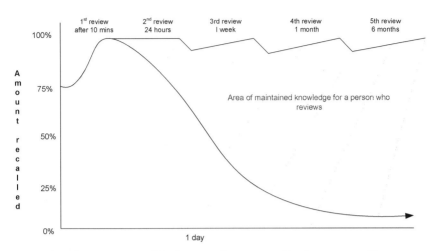

Graph of amount of information recalled versus time lapse. Information recalled is higher for a person who reviews than for the one who does not, with increase in time lapse.

Exam and Test Preparation

Whether it is a routine test or end-of-session exams, the thought of an impending assessment usually fills most people with dread.

This feeling does not dissipate even if one has been preparing for months in advance. It is simply born out of a dread of failure.

Some steps you can take to help you get better prepared are as follows:

- **First things first:** Be realistic about your state of preparedness. Have you been busy with every other thing but your books? This is not the time to feel guilty, but to make a realistic evaluation of how ready you are, and decide what to do to improve your chances of success.

- **<u>Do something about it:</u>** After realizing how prepared (or unprepared) you are and deciding on what to do about it, don't wait another second. Go ahead and do it immediately.

- **<u>Focus on the key areas of the syllabus:</u>** Read the core areas of the syllabus and skip the less important areas. Focus on only what is necessary for the exams or test. This is not the time to read the entire material from cover to cover.

- **<u>Practice previous questions:</u>** when it comes to passing examinations, there is only one way to get there- by practicing lots of previous questions.
The more questions you practice, especially if you time yourself as you practice them, the fairer your chances of passing the exams.
Experience shows that, for major exams, questions are often repeated from previous years, but with slight

modifications which a trained eye can easily detect.

However, in practicing previous questions, you must apply a measure of discipline. Resist the temptation of checking the answer before you answer the question fully.

Only check the answer after you have completed the question and you want to check whether you answered it correctly or not.

Checking the answers without answering the questions first will do nothing to prepare you for the exams, and even if that same question comes up, you will be unable to answer it correctly because you have not gone through the process in your mind.

Design a 'mock exam' for yourself, by selecting some questions from similar exams taken in previous years. Attempt the questions under exam conditions (you can use an alarm clock for this); and stop when the recommended time is up. Mark your work using the answers provided to see how you score. Then find out why you got some of the questions wrong, if any, so that you can avoid making the same mistakes during the actual exams.

Do this 'mock' practice at least three times before the exams. If you pass these successfully, you will surely excel in the actual exams.

If there are no past questions, try to understand your lecturer or teacher. They always give away their questions in class, and usually disguise them as practice questions or assignments. They may also give hints of the potential source of the questions. It is therefore important that you attend all your classes, from the first to last.

Keys for effective test and exam taking

- **Rest adequately:** As mentioned in the previous chapter, you need to know if you are an early bird or a night owl. Whichever category you may belong, never underestimate the importance of getting proper sleep before your exam. Studies show that we are most creative and effective when we are well rested. Manage your time effectively to ensure that you have the time to rest.

- **Follow the instructions given:** Where the question says state, state! If it says define, do just that-define! When it says explain, you must go all out to explain to the best of your ability.
  A more detailed explanation of the kind of questions to expect at your level and how to answer them, is provided under output skills.

- **Attempt all questions:** The more questions you answer in an exam, the more marks you will get.
  Therefore try to answer the full number of questions required of you in an exam,

even if you cannot answer all of them completely.

- **<u>Revising at the exam hall:</u>** Don't attempt to revise everything in the exam hall. When you get in there, be calm, and avoid any sort of panic.
Instead be calm, go over your key points again, try to strengthen your weak spots, and listen to other people discuss. You may pick up a thing or two from them.

- **<u>After the exams:</u>** Celebrate, and avoid cross-examining your answers with your colleagues. You have done your best, so leave it at that. Your results will tell if you did well or not.

Handling failure

If, when the results come, you find that you failed, do not lose hope.

Realise that failing is different from being a failure, even when you fail often.

You only become a failure when you stop trying to be a success, or when you refuse to do something about your past failures.

Do not under any circumstance blame the examining body. Even though there is a slight chance that they are to blame, they are right over 98 percent of the time.

Realize that the responsibility for your failure or success lies squarely on your shoulders, so it is up to you to ensure that you succeed the next time you try.

Failing is something that can happen to any person for a variety of reasons. No body likes it, but it does happen, even to the best.

You can turn your failure into success by doing the following:

- Know that you can change it. You are not helpless.

- Identify the root cause. What are you doing wrong? Is it that you are not resting properly, not managing your time well, not answering your questions correctly, or not studying properly?

- Accept responsibility for your poor performance. As long as you keep blaming someone else, such as your family, the examining body, or your teachers/lecturers, you will never succeed.

- Decide to change it by following the principles laid out in this book, and you will succeed.

Output skills

Taking tests and exams

Test/exam taking

When writing an exam, answer the questions presented to you, and not what you think the question should be.

Now there are several levels of questions which should be asked a student, according to the six degrees of difficulties which must be mastered in the area of learning.

These levels and their meanings are shown in the following tables (sourced from http://www. skagitwatershed.org/~donclark/hrd/bloom. html:)

Table 3.

Category	Example and Key words
Knowledge*: Simply recall data or information*	**Example:** Recite a policy. Define Photosynthesis. **Key Words:** Define, describe, identify, know, label, list, match, name, outline, recall, recognize, reproduce, select, state.
Comprehension*: Understand the meaning, translation, interpolation, and interpretation of instructions and problems. State a problem in one's own words.*	**Examples**: Rewrites the principles of test writing. Explain in one's own words the steps for performing a complex task. Translate an equation into a computer spreadsheet. **Key Words**: comprehends, converts, defends, distinguishes, estimates, explains, extends, generalizes, gives Examples, infers, interprets, paraphrases, predicts, rewrites, summarizes, translates.
Application*: Use a concept in a new situation or unprompted use of an abstraction. Applies what was learned in the classroom into novel situations in the work place.*	**Examples**: Use a manual to calculate an employee's vacation time. Apply laws of statistics to evaluate the reliability of a written test. **Key Words**: applies, changes, computes, constructs, demonstrates, discovers, manipulates, modifies, operates, predicts, prepares, produces, relates, shows, solves, uses.

Category	Example and Key words
Analysis*: Separates material or concepts into component parts so that its organizational structure may be understood. Distinguishes between facts and inferences.*	**Examples**: Troubleshoot a piece of equipment by using logical deduction. Recognize logical fallacies in reasoning. Gather information from a department and select the required tasks for training. **Key Words**: analyzes, breaks down, compares, contrasts, diagrams, deconstructs, differentiates, discriminates, distinguishes, identifies, illustrates, infers, outlines, relates, selects, separates.
Synthesis*: Builds a structure or pattern from diverse elements. Put parts together to form a whole, with emphasis on creating a new meaning or structure.*	**Examples**: Write a company operations or process manual. Design a machine to perform a specific task. Integrates training from several sources to solve a problem. Revise and process to improve the outcome. **Key Words**: categorizes, combines, compiles, composes, creates, devises, designs, explains, generates, modifies, organizes, plans, rearranges, reconstructs, relates, reorganizes, revises, rewrites, summarizes, tells, writes.

Category	Example and Key words
Evaluation: Make judgments about the value of ideas or materials.	**Examples**: Select the most effective solution. Hire the most qualified candidate. Explain and justify a new budget. **Key Words**: appraises, compares, concludes, contrasts, criticizes, critiques, defends, describes, discriminates, evaluates, explains, interprets, justifies, relates, summarizes, supports.

4

Your Personal Development Plan

Just like the muscles of your body, your brain needs exercise to develop all its faculties and function optimally.

Things you can do to exercise your mental faculties and stimulate them to healthy development and creative expression are as follows:

1. Believe in Yourself.

The exam hall usually reveals how much we truly believe in our own abilities.
It has been observed that the less confident students try to get ahead by copying, while the more confident ones try to think it through and tackle the questions, come what may.

The latter group have learned to believe in their ability because they have exercised it at some point. Note that each academic victory you have won, only prepares you for the next academic challenge you may face in future, such as higher academic degrees.

Copying when you are stuck may seem like the smart thing to do, but its effect on the brain is like drinking poison.

Copying kills the desire of the brain to initiate its own ideas, thus destroying its abilities and potentials.

Therefore, lay aside every fear of failure and try to do things on your own. Develop your hidden potentials and enjoy the rich dividends of your labour and development.
Success earned this way tastes sweeter, last longer, and gives birth to even more success in every area of your life and future endeavours.

2. Read Far and Wide.
Someone said, "Readers are leaders". If there is anything that will put you ahead of others in your chosen field of study, it is that extra knowledge you have that no one else has. And the major way to get this extra knowledge is by reading. Therefore read as much as you can and as often as you can.

3. Keep the Passion Alive.

Reading something about your area of interest at least once a month, will keep your interest in that area burning strong and gaining ground. But if you neglect it for too long, the passion will begin to die out, taking with it any development or success you may have had in that area.

4. Read Personal Development Materials at least once every month.

This will help you develop your potentials and boost your confidence to tackle challenges.

5.Take a course on Speed Reading

Reading faster will save you a lot of time and give you room to read more books.

6. Learn to Communicate Better.

Try to be good at the language in which you are learning, and learn to express yourself correctly in that language, for example, English, French, or Arabic. If you cannot communicate effectively in the language in which you are learning, you cannot succeed in your studies even if you have the correct answers because you cannot communicate those correct answers effectively.

7. Be Fluent In a Global Language

Determine to be fluent in a second language that is recognised all over the world, such as English, Spanish, French or Arabic. This will open you up to new areas of learning, as well as new opportunities for success and self-development.

Biblography

- Buzan T. *Use Your Head* Guild publishing, London 1984.

- Wycoff J. *Mindmapping* Berkley Books, London 1991.

- Montgomery R. *Memory Power* Learn incorporated 1985.

- Luckie W. & Smethurst W. *Study Power* Bookline Books 1998.

- www.medscape.com

- www.thoughtfueled.com

- www.skagitwatershed.org